George Frideric
HANDEL

MY HEART IS INDITING
Coronation Anthem IV
HWV 261

Arranged by

Friedrich Chrysander

Edited by

Clark McAlister

Vocal Score
Klavierauszug

SERENISSIMA MUSIC, INC.

PREFACE

This edition of Handel's *Coronation Anthems* is based upon that of Friedrich Chrysander for the first Handel-Gesellschaft. We have accepted his basic text of these works, choosing only to revise and clarify it in the following aspects:

1. Suggestions for optional overdotting, according to our general understanding of baroque performance practice. These overdottings are shown above the first staff of each score system, and should be applied to those voices and/or instruments within that system as appropriate. These optional overdottings, when appropriate, are shown in the parts and in the vocal score which accompanies this revised edition in the same manner.

2. Tacit correction of a few errors of pitch and obvious inconsistencies of rhythm.

3. Clarification of the use of bassoons within the bass-line group of instruments. The bassoon parts which accompany this revised score have been prepared according to the principles set forth by Adam Carse in *The Orchestra in the XVIII Century*.

4. Preparation of a keyboard realization of Handel's figured bass. The original version of this edition of these anthems included only a keyboard reduction of the orchestral texture prepared by Im. Faisst, which of course is not what is required for stylistic performance of this music. The performance material for this revised edition includes a realization for organ of the figured bass.

Clark McAlister
August, 1986

VERSES

Duration: ca.9-10 minutes

Composed August-September 1727
First performance: October 22, 1727
London, Westminster Abbey
Coronation of King George II
Chapel Royal Soli, Chorus, Orchestra, Composer (conductor)

ISBN: 978-1-60874-205-9

MY HEART IS INDITING

HWV 261

George Frideric Handel
Arranged by Friedrich Chrysander
Edited by Clark McAlister

Soprano

Alto II — Solo

My heart is is in - dit - ing, my

Tenor

Bass I — Solo

My heart is in - dit - ing, my

SERENISSIMA MUSIC, INC.

27 heart is in - dit - ing of a good mat - ter; I speak

heart is in - dit - ing of a good mat - ter; I

32 of the things which I have made

speak of the things which I have

36 un - to the King, which I have made un - to the King, which I have

made, which I have made un - to the King, which I have

40

Solo

My

made un-to the King.

made un-to the King.

f

[tr] [tr]

46

heart is in - dit - ing,   my heart is in -

Solo

My heart is in - dit - ing,   my heart is in -

p

51

dit - ing of a good mat - ter;   I speak

dit - ing of a good mat - ter;   I speak   of the

56
of the things which I have made,
things which I have made un-to the
60
which I have made un-to the King, which I have made un-to the
1st Alto
I
King, which I have made un-to the King, which I have made un-to the
I
64
King.
I
speak of the things which I have
King.
I
I speak of the things

68
speak of the things which I - have
made, which I have made un-to the King, which I have
speak of the things which I have
which I have made un-to the King,

72
[f] Chorus
made un - to the King. My heart is in - dit - ing, my heart is in -
Alto I
[f] Chorus
made un-to the King. My heart is in - dit - ing, my heart is in -
Alto II
[f] Chorus
My heart is in - dit - ing, my heart is in -
[f] Chorus
made un-to the King. My heart is in - dit - ing, my heart is in -
Bass I
[f] Chorus
My heart is in - dit - ing, my heart is in -
Bass II
[f] Chorus
My heart is in dit ing, my heart is in -
[f]

dit - ing, my heart is in - dit - ing, in - dit - ing, in - dit - ing of

a good mat - ter; I speak

a good mat - ter; I speak of the

a good mat - ter; I speak of the

a good mat - ter; I speak

Bass I & II

a good mat - ter; I speak

86
Alto I & II
of the things, of the things,
things, I speak of the things, which I have
of the things, I speak of the things
of the things, of the things,
90
which I have made un - to the King, which I have made
made un - to the King, which I have made
which I have made un - to the King, which I have made
which I have made un - to the King, which I have made
95
un-to the King.
un - to the King.
un - to the King.
un - to the King.
tr

Andante

[mf]

104

107

[cresc.]

[f]

110 Soprano Solo

Kings' daugh-ters   were a - mong thy hon -

[p]

[f]

[p]

113

- our a - ble wo-men,

Alto I Solo

Kings' daugh - ters were a - mong thy hon -

116
were a - mong thy hon-our - a-ble wo -
- our - a - ble — wo - men,
were a -
119
men.
mong thy hon-our - a - ble wo - men.
[f] Chorus
Kings' daugh-ters,
Tenor
[f] Chorus
Kings' daugh - ters,
Bass I & II
Chorus
[f]
Kings' daugh - ters,
Kings' daugh-ters,
[f]
122
[f] Chorus
Kings' daugh-ters
were a - mong thy hon-our - a - ble wo -
Alto I
Kings' daugh - ters
were a - mong thy hon-our - a - ble wo -
[f] Alto II Chorus
Kings' daugh - ters
were a - mong thy hon-our - a - ble wo -
Kings' daugh-ters
were a - mong thy hon-our a - ble wo -
Kings' daugh-ters,
Kings' daugh-ters were a - mong thy hon - our - a - ble

125
men, were a - mong thy hon-our - a -
men, were a - mong thy hon-our - a -
men, were a - mong thy hon - our a -
men, were a - mong thy hon - our a -
wo - men, were a - mong thy hon - our - a -
128
ble wo - men, Kings' daugh-ters, Kings' daugh-ters were a -
ble wo - men, Kings' daugh-ters, Kings' daugh-ters were a - mong, a -
ble wo - men, Kings' daugh-ters, Kings' daugh-ters were a - mong, a -
ble wo - men, Kings' daugh-ters, Kings' daugh-ters were a - mong, a -
ble wo - men, Kings' daugh-ters, Kings' daugh-ters were a -

131
mong thy hon - our - a-ble wo - men, Kings' daugh - ters, Kings' daugh-ters,
mong thy hon - our-a - ble wo - men, Kings' daugh-ters, Kings' daugh-ters,
mong thy hon - our-a - ble wo - men, Kings' daugh - ters,
mong thy hon - our - a - ble wo - men, Kings' daugh - ters,
mong thy hon - our - a-ble wo - men, Kings' daugh-ters, Kings' daugh-ters,
134
Kings' daugh-ters, Kings' daugh-ters Kings' daugh -ters, were a - mong thy hon -
Kings' daugh-ters, Kings' daugh - ters were a -
Kings' daugh-ters, Kings' daugh - ters
Kings' daugh-ters, Kings, daugh-ters, Kings' daugh-ters, Kings' daugh-ters
Kings' daugh - ters, Kings, daugh-ters, Kings, daugh-ters

137
- our - a - ble wo - men, a - mong thy hon - our - a - ble wo - men, were a -
mong thy hon - our - a - ble wo - men, a - mong thy hon - our - a - ble wo - men, were a -
were a - mong thy hon - our - a - ble wo - men, were a -
were a - mong thy hon - our - a - ble wo - men, were a -
were a - mong thy hon - our - a - ble wo - men, were a -
140
mong, were a - mong thy hon - our - a - ble wo - men.
mong thy hon - our - a - ble wo - men.
mong thy hon - our - a - ble wo - men.
mong thy hon - our - a - ble wo - men.
mong thy hon - our - a - ble wo - men.
tr
143

Andante
[p]
159
[f]
160
[p]
166
Soprano
Solo
Up - on thy right hand
Alto I
Solo
Up - on thy right hand
Alto II
Tenor
Bass

did stand the Queen, in ves-ture of gold,_____

did stand the Queen, in ves-ture of gold,_____

Solo
Up - on thy right hand did stand the Queen in

Solo
Up - on thy right hand did stand the Queen in

Solo
Up - on thy right hand did stand the Queen in

Solo
Up - on thy right hand did stand the Queen in

185
[f] Chorus
and the King shall have
ves - ture of gold;
[f] Chorus
and the King shall have
ves - ture of gold;
[f] Chorus
and the King shall have
ves - ture of gold;
[f] Chorus
and the King shall have
ves - ture of gold;
[f] Chorus
and the King shall have
[f]
191
pleas - ure, pleas - ure, pleas - ure, and the King shall have
pleas - ure, the King shall have pleas - ure, pleas - ure,
pleas - ure, pleas - ure, pleas - ure, the King shall have pleas -
pleas - ure, pleas - ure, the King shall have pleas - ure, pleas - ure,
pleas - ure, shall have pleas -

197
pleas - ure, pleas - ure,
pleas-ure, pleas-ure, shall have pleas-ure, pleas - ure,
ure, pleas-ure, shall have pleas-ure, pleas - ure,
pleas-ure, pleas-ure, shall have pleas-ure, pleas - ure,
ure, pleas - ure,
[p]
[f]
203
the King shall have pleas - ure in thy beau - ty.
the King shall have pleas - ure in thy beau - ty.
the King shall have pleas - ure in thy beau - ty.
the King shall have pleas - ure in thy beau - ty.
the King shall have pleas - ure in thy beau - ty.
tr
tr

209
[f]
Up - on thy right hand did stand the Queen, in
215
ves - ture of gold; the King shall have pleas - ure, the King shall have
ves - ture of gold; the King shall have pleas - ure,
ves - ture of gold; the King shall have pleas -
ves - ture of gold;

220

pleas - _____ ure, pleas - ure, pleas - ure, the

pleas - ure, shall have pleas - ure, the King shall have pleas - _____

_____ ure, shall have pleas - ure, pleas - ure, pleas - _____

_____ ure, shall have pleas - ure, pleas - ure, pleas - ure, the

the King shall have pleas - _____ ure,

225

King shall have pleas - ure, pleas - ure, the King shall have pleas - ure in

_____ ure, pleas - ure, the King shall have pleas - ure in

_____ ure, the King shall have pleas - ure in

King shall have pleas - ure, pleas - ure, the King shall have pleas - ure in

pleas - ure, pleas - ure, pleas - ure, the King shall have pleas - ure in

230
thy beau - ty, the King shall have pleas - ure, pleas - ure,
thy beau - ty, the King shall have pleas - ure, pleas - ure,
thy beau - ty, the King shall have pleas - ure, pleas - ure,
thy beau - ty, the King shall have pleas - ure, pleas - ure,
thy beau - ty, the King shall have pleas - ure, pleas - ure,
[p]
236
[f]
the King shall have pleas - ure in thy beau - ty.
[f]
the King shall have pleas - ure in thy beau - ty.
[f]
the King shall have pleas - ure in thy beau - ty.
[f]
the King shall have pleas-ure in thy beau - ty.
[f]
the King shall have pleas-ure in thy beau - ty.
[f]
[p]
242

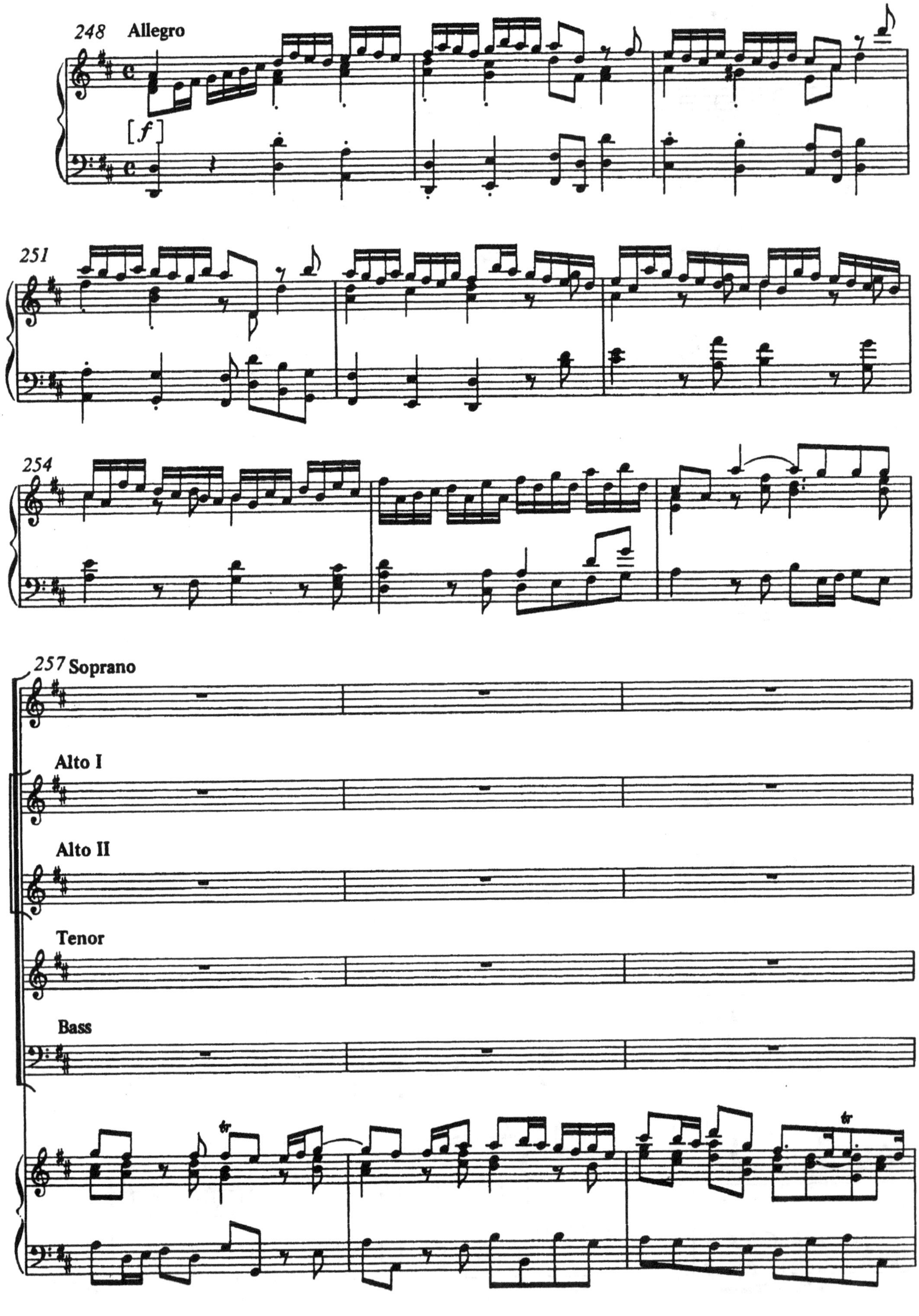
248 Allegro
[f]
251
254
257 Soprano
Alto I
Alto II
Tenor
Bass
tr

260
[f]
Kings, Kings shall be thy nurs - ing fa - thers,
Kings, Kings shall be thy nurs - ing fa - thers,
Kings, Kings shall be thy nurs - ing fa- thers,
Kings, Kings, shall be thy nurs - ing fa- thers,
Kings, Kings, shall be thy nurs - ing fa- thers,
263
[simile]
Kings shall be thy nurs - ing fa –
Kings shall be thy nurs - ing fa –
Kings shall be thy

266

thers,   thy
thers, thy nurs - ing fa - thers,   thy
nurs - ing fa - thers,   thy
thy nurs - ing fa -
thy nurs - ing fa -

269

nurs - ing fa - thers, thy nurs - ing fa -
thy nurs - ing fa -
nurs - ing fa - thers, thy nurs - ing fa -
thers, thy nurs - ing fa -
thers, thy nurs - ing fa -

272

thers, and queens, and queens thy nurs- ing

thers, and

thers, and queens thy nurs-ing mo- thers, thy nurs - ing mo -

thers,

thers,

275

mo - thers, and queens thy nurs-ing mo- thers, thy nurs - ing mo -

queens thy nurs - ing mo-

thers,

and queens, and queens thy nurs - ing mo-thers, and queens thy nurs-ing

278
thers, kings shall be thy nurs - ing fa -
thers, kings shall be thy nurs - ing fa -
kings, kings shall be thy nurs - ing fa -
mo - thers, kings shall be thy nurs - ing fa -
kings, kings shall be thy nurs - ing fa -
tr
281
thers, and queens, and queens thy nurs - ing, nurs - ing
thers, and queens, and queens thy nurs -
thers, and queens, and queens thy nurs -
thers,
thers, and queens thy nurs - ing mo - thers, thy nurs - ing

284
mo - thers, and queens, and queens thy
ing mo - thers, and queens thy nurs-ing mo - thers, and queens thy nurs - ing
ing mo - thers, and queens thy nurs-ing mo - thers, and queens thy nurs - ing
and queens thy nurs - ing mo- thers, and
mo - thers, and queens, and queens, and queens thy nurs - ing mo -
287
nurs - ing mo - thers, and queens thy nurs - ing
mo-thers, thy nurs - ing mo - thers, and queens thy nurs-ing mo-
mo-thers, thy nurs - ing mo - thers, and queens thy nurs - ing
queens thy nurs - ing mo - thers, and queens thy nurs - ing
thers, thy nurs - ing mo - thers, and queens thy nurs - ing
tr

296
queens, and queens thy nurs - ing mo - thers, kings,
queens, and queens thy nurs - ing mo - thers, kings,
queens, and queens thy nurs - ing mo - thers, kings,
queens, and queens thy nurs - ing mo - thers, kings,
queens thy nurs - ing mo – thers, kings,
299
[ff]
kings, kings, kings, kings shall be thy nurs - ing
[ff]
kings, kings, kings, kings shall be thy
[ff]
kings, kings, kings, kings shall be thy
[ff]
kings, kings, kings, kings, shall be thy
[ff]
kings, kings, kings, kings shall be thy
[ff]

302

fa - thers, shall be thy nurs - ing

nurs - ing fa - thers, shall be thy nurs - ing

nurs - ing fa - thers, shall be thy nurs - ing

nurs - ing fa - thers, shall be thy nurs - ing

nurs - ing fa - thers, shall be thy nurs - ing

305

fa - thers, and queens, and queens thy nurs - ing

fa - thers, and queens, and queens thy nurs - ing mo -

fa - thers, and queens, and queens thy nurs - ing

fa - thers, and queens, and queens thy nurs - ing

fa - thers, and queens, and queens thy nurs - ing

308
mo - thers, kings, kings shall be thy nurs - ing fa - thers, thy
thers, kings, kings shall be thy nurs - ing fa - thers, thy
mo - thers, kings, kings shall be thy nurs - ing fa - thers, thy
mo - thers, kings, kings shall be thy nurs - ing fa - thers, thy
mo - thers, kings, kings shall be thy nurs - ing fa - thers, thy
311
nurs - ing fa - thers, and queens thy nurs - ing
nurs - ing fa - thers, and queens thy nurs - ing
nurs - ing fa - thers, and queens thy nurs - ing
nurs - ing fa - thers, and queens thy nurs - ing
nurs - ing fa - thers, and queens thy nurs - ing

314
mo - thers, and queens thy nurs - ing mo - thers, and
317 Adagio
queens thy nurs - ing mo - - thers.
queens thy___ nurs - ing mo - - thers.
Adagio
Ped.

www.ingramcontent.com/pod-product-compliance
Lightning Source LLC
Chambersburg PA
CBHW081601040426
42445CB00025B/1780